# Where Men Dare Not Tread

Shawn Boutilier

ISBN 978-1-7387031-0-4

# FORWARD

Years ago, I was in meetings every Friday night in a prophetic church. The church was part of Christian International Network of Apostles and Prophets, Bill Hamon's people. It seemed on the cutting edge for the prophetic in Edmonton. I didn't find anywhere else that compared. They allowed people to prophesy, according to how they were led by the Lord.

Being new to the church, I knew some people, but was still trying to fit in. One Friday, the Holy Spirit gave me a vision, which they said I could share. The Lord showed everyone in the church elevated off the floor, with their heads were up against the ceiling. The Lord then said the church had been through a number of things the last couple of years. He told me the ceiling represented the trials, tests, and problems we endure as believers. That if they persevered they would break through the ceiling into a new realm of God and a new anointing of the church.

But alas, they seemed to disregard what I shared and realized I did my part in proclaiming it. But the Lord made it known to me that day that believers suffered many things, especially if they have high callings on their lives. Nobody who is anointed gets there without suffering through a number of things.

I recall hearing Gary Oates start a pastor's conference years ago. He said, "The longer someone is in the wilderness, the stronger the calling, the more trials they endure, the more powerful the anointing."

This book is about thirty years of enduring much pain and trials while God revealed His plan to me. First and foremost, my purpose in writing this is that the Lord told me to do it. I hope it speaks to you.

# TABLE OF CONTENTS

# INTRODUCTION

"Whatever a man sows, that he will reap." - Gal 6:7

I was at a meeting with the school of the supernatural at Lighthouse Church in Stony Plain, Alberta. The pastor who led the school, Pastor Tim Ulmer, was praying for a lady in need of healing. Everyone was praying with someone, and I stood alone.

Immediately, in an open vision, I was in Heaven and could see an Angel about twenty feet tall, made of fire, standing behind where the pastor was ministering. I could see Heaven and the normal world at the same time.

As I turned to look, I could see in Heaven what looked like giant steps. I started looking upwards, where I saw many steps, one above the other. At the very top, the Lord sat upon a throne. Suddenly, I was looking through His eyes.

Ephesians 2:6 "has raised us up together and made us sit together in Heavenly places in Christ Jesus." Over the years, God has done this to me; when you're looking through His eyes, you know His heart. It is in these times God gives me revelation in His word or about His ways. The Lord looked throughout the earth, and he would watch as Christians tried to minister to people. For the eyes of the Lord search the whole earth to strengthen those whose hearts are fully committed to him; the Lord was earnestly waiting for believers to step out and help others.

The Holy Spirit showed me Noah's Ark and how God instructed him to build it to exact measurements. He showed me Moses making the Tabernacle of meeting according to God's specific details. God then showed me King David, who was inspired how to build Solomon's Temple by the Spirit. The Lord can show you these things rapidly, almost as if He is downloading this revelation into you.

Next, the Holy Spirit showed me Paul proclaiming the Old Testament was a shadow of heavenly things. The Lord said that as we step out in faith to minister and do things that look Heavenly, God would show up in power, and the ministering Angels would enter the scene. Prophetic people use to call it framing, that you would step into a place where God operates. No wonder Jesus said, I only do what I see, the things my Father is doing. I wait on the Lord and look to see what the Father is doing. Then, I act out what He shows me. The results are God moving in miracles when I follow His lead.

It is not enough to move in faith and do what we've always done. His Spirit leads them who are the Sons of God. I see ministers operating on a hit-and-miss principle—almost a methodological way of doing things. God wants us to follow the Spirit, and he performs the miracles. This experience reveals that God's Kingdom operates in exact detail and brings extraordinary results. God desired His children to reach out so He could touch a hurting world. I could feel His heart's yearning for any of us to take a step of faith that He may come to show himself to us, and in you. This vision gave me an understanding that His Kingdom comes to earth when we do precisely what the Holy Spirit is doing. Secondly, that as I share with you testimonies of what He has done. That as I share with you for God's glory that you would reap the same experiences and never be the same. Praise God!

Romans 10:17: "So then faith comes by hearing and hearing by the word of God." As you listen to the testimonies of this book, God will visit you.

# EARLY YEARS

I was born on October 3rd, 1966, in East York Hospital, a borough of the greater Toronto Area. My first seven years were uneventful until we moved to a new area. Upon arrival, I immediately ran into trouble with multiple children of different ages, experienced a lot of bullying, and had groups of kids chasing me home several times.

When I was seven, I developed my first crush on a neighborhood girl, Rosy. I found out she was being driven to Sunday school by a church elder at a highway gospel church. Even though I was Catholic, my mother let me go to this church. I now believe this was God's hand in planting the seed of His Word in my heart.

Our Sunday school teachers would ask us to invite Jesus into our hearts, even if we didn't understand yet the meaning. Mr. Goodyear, a church elder, was loved by all the neighborhood kids. A bunch of us went to see him one day. He asked me to step forward in front of the other kids, to lay hands on me and start prophesying on me.

Another one of the kids asked if the rest could receive prayer.

In response, Mr. Goodyear said, "No, the Holy Spirit said to call out Shawn."

I didn't understand what this meant at the time. Never underestimate God's ability to reach someone chosen as His.

Through the next couple of years, I continued to be harassed by the same kids. When I was twelve, I met a friend named Stuart, a Catholic boy. For some reason, he asked me to go several times to a full Gospel Baptist Church. I did so, and immediately noticed God's presence in this church, whose pastor said he'd had a visitation in Heaven. The church had a large painting on the wall depicting what he'd seen; it showed the father sitting on the throne as a large ghosted figure in a robe. God had His right arm pointing downwards to a smaller throne, which had Jesus on it. Where the father's hand should be, it flowed into Jesus' person, making them one. Here, Jesus was actually God's right hand.

Visiting this church caused me to experiencc visions. Two of them were very crucial to me in understanding God.

In the first one, I was in Heaven, and I saw the Heavenly Father sitting in a courtroom with multitudes of people lined up; God was sitting in a judge's stand. In my vision, He would reach down toward people and turn them towards Him while lifting them off the ground. Then, he would start to prophesy over them, declaring their names, where they would be born, their future occupations, and calling on their lives. The Holy Spirit showed me they would then be sent to Earth to be born as babies. Everything that was prophesied was written into His books. This was around the late '70s, and no one talked about the courts of Heaven during these days or preached doctrine that I saw in this vision.

The other vision happened when the pastor was preaching about the apostles abandoning Jesus at the cross. All of a sudden, I saw myself sitting in a cell with Jesus. He was waiting to be judged by Pilate, his long dark hair hung heavy with sweat matted to his head. He was staring straight ahead as I was telling him, "I will never leave you, Jesus. I will never leave you!"

He never said a word, but kept looking forward.

These visions stick with me to this day, with how vividly God was trying to show me His presence in my life. Yet, despite all of this, I still turned to the ways of the world. I spent the next five years taking karate to protect myself against bullies. Years of abuse caused me to harden into an angry young man. I fell into drugs and alcohol to fit in with those who chased me.

My change was significant enough that when I saw Mr. Goodyear, he said to me, "You've gone after the ways of the world, boy."

My partying became so severe that I'm pretty sure I overdosed twice due to mixing substances. My heart rate had also reached over 150 beats per minute both times, and when this happened, I thought I would suffer from a heart attack. Though I wasn't yet serving God, I still called out to Him to be merciful and not let me die.

At this time in my life, I began a new chapter as a pipefitter apprentice. One time, when I was working on a job site, The Holy Spirit tried to reach me again. My father was my foreman, and he was asking me to put in hangers with a 14-foot ladder. Once at the top of the ladder, I was assessing the job, though people suggest you don't stand on the top two rungs for a reason. Sure enough, the ladder shifted and was about to topple over, and I reached out to grab small pipes on either side of me. My holding them completed the circuit, and I could feel electricity flow throughout my body, to the point that I thought my blood was boiling in my arms. My brain was aware of what was happening the entire time, knowing I was being electrocuted.

Two invisible hands grabbed my calves and abruptly pushed me off the ladder, breaking the circuit. The force made me go headfirst through a T-bar ceiling. I could hear my Dad call out my name ("Shawn!"). Suddenly, it seemed time and space stood still as God caused me to hover in the air for a couple of seconds, and I could hear His voice speak clearly in my head, saying, "Tuck in your shoulder."

Then, time and everything started moving again, and I continued to fall, my left knee hitting a wooden chair, which broke into two. My tucked-in shoulder hit the concrete floor, the momentum allowing me to roll back onto my feet.

I had fallen over nineteen feet to the ground. A coworker came running toward me, saying if he hadn't seen my fall happen, he wouldn't have believed it. He told me that I had gone through the ceiling, hit the chair, and landed back on my feet. He exclaimed, "I wish I had a video camera because that was impossible!"

For several months, I would walk by that office, wondering who had pushed me off that ladder. Praise God!

In any event, being electrocuted and overdosing made me think God was trying to tell me something. At 25 years of age, and about 12 years of partying, it occurred to me that God was trying to get my attention.

On the same job, a supervisor was trying to lift equipment that weighed a couple of tons. They had a pallet jack on one side with several small car jacks on two sides. He asked me to grab something, and he was extremely hard of hearing. I told him to wait, but he let it down quickly; the unit fell several feet and landed on two one-inch tabs on the jacks. Everything rocked; it should kick the jacks out and severed my hand clean off. But once again, God was protecting me.

God continued to try getting my attention with yet another event, which was celebrating a friend's bachelor party. As we drank and did drugs all night, they convinced a friend of ours to drive. I protested and got into a fight with a friend, knocking him out cold. They carried him to the car and we drove. Sure enough, we were hit by an 18-wheeler truck on highway 401. My friend who was driving had swerved into the trucker's lane, and the big truck hit us from behind.

I was sitting in the back, and I observed our vehicle became airborne and lifted off the ground. My friend Bill was driving, and I saw him grab the steering wheel tightly with both hands; he was going to slam on the brakes. But instead, he screamed, "No!" and slammed his foot to the floor beside the gas pedal—not the brake. He later told me the thought came to him instantly; if he had slammed on the brakes, the car would have flipped due to the force of the truck hitting us from behind. When Bill had grabbed the steering wheel, it seemed again God had slowed time to give him enough time to react—showing time and time again that a supernatural God intervenes in the affairs of men. When God wants to save your children, He and the Kingdom of Heaven's forces are always calling out to the lost. There is hope for your lost Sons and Daughters because He never gives up.

Still, my life was a mess. I was arrested for drug possession twice, had been through several girlfriends, and was always getting into fights. I was unhappy with many things in my life. I only wanted to find someone to love me so that I could love her. I tried making money in multi-level marketing, but God sovereignly used this endeavor for me to meet Brian, a new friend. For some reason, this Catholic Irish man asked me to go to a Pentecostal church. As I write this, it strikes me how God used Rosy, Stuart, and Brian to show Himself to me. He had people inviting me to church, and my relationships with these people centered on worldly things, yet he used them for me—what a merciful God.

When I went with Brian to Pentecostal church, a man stood and started speaking in tongues. A peace that surpassed understanding permeated the atmosphere of the church. Fire came down and lit up my spirit; I stood mesmerized, looking at the man speaking. "What was that I asked Brian?" He explained that he was speaking in Tongues! I thought about that presence of Peace and knew this is what I was looking for in my life. I told Brian that I was coming back next week. He was also interested in coming back. The following week at church, I saw a bulletin about baptism on the church newsletter, which described the importance of public confession of one's faith. I told Brian my decision, and he decided to join me. I still don't understand how God got me to this part of my journey.

Over the following months, I started reading my Bible and learning about the miracles of Jesus. I heard preachers talk about healing and miracles, and my heart burned to see those things. I was still drinking on weekends and partying, but now I was starting to really look at the workings of God.

I met a new friend in an older lady named Elizabeth, who was instrumental in my journey to seek the more extraordinary things in the kingdom. I struggled with whether I should go partying on New Year's Eve or go to a watch night service at a new church I was attending. I told Brian, and he was thinking the same thing. So, we decided to go to church together. Again, something burned in my heart that night, and I prayed while the people around me were worshipping.

"Lord," I said, "if you show me that all these things are true about miracles, healings, and the supernatural, I will give you the next year of my life. I declare I will try with all I got to seek you."

Well, God honored that statement.

# CALLING

In 1993, I was invited to a Mike Murdoch meeting in Baltimore. I was praying to be baptized in the Holy Spirit. I was with a Reverend Larry Lee (a Chinese pastor, not the other one!) and three sisters. One was my new friend Elizabeth, who was like a Spiritual mom to me.

I was in a minivan and reading a Bible. The Devil kept condemning me about the scripture, Matthew 7:23: "And then I will declare to them, I never knew you; depart from me you who practice lawlessness." In response, I was calling out to the Lord in prayer.

We arrived in Baltimore the night before the conference. After checking into the room, I realized that I left my Bible at home. I found a Gideon's Bible in the room and quickly read Psalm 91, as I'd heard a lady preaching on Psalm 91 for protection over your life.

I got up early in the morning to pray, as I have always done, being taught by intercessors, "If we abide in him, he abides in us." In the morning service, after some great worship, Mike gave his message. In those days, he preached a lot on wisdom out of Proverbs.

Later that evening, we returned for another service, and God had something different in mind. Mike started walking back and forth, saying God was calling someone in the service to the ministry. He walked up to me and looked at me, and I didn't respond; I didn't feel the need to be seen by men. Elizabeth started bumping me with her arm and saying, "It's you, it's you." But for some reason, I didn't step forward.

Suddenly, heat and electricity came over me, and I saw a large glass flask, the size of a man, being filled with golden oil to the top.

I was in a daze for the rest of the service. After the service, I returned to my room for the night and went to sleep on a king-sized bed. I dreamt I was in Heaven. It was as if I was physically there, standing before God on His throne, and millions of Angels stood around with beasts who worshipped God. I had my back to Him, yet I was standing very close to Him. Somehow, I knew I couldn't turn around and look at him as He was, but He spoke so clearly, there was no mistaking what he said: "Man's words are not your words!"

As He said this, I saw an image of Mike Murdoch hovering beside me as the Lord emphasized that man's words weren't mine. Then, He declared more loudly, "Your words are not my words!" and continued even louder, "My words are your words." He said again with Authority, "My words are your words." Then for a third time, He declared with His voice so loudly and with such Authority, it thundered in the Heavens. Everything shook with might, and the Heavenly Host broke out in praise—"Holy, Holy, Holy, Holy." Their combined voices blended so perfectly that they sounded like a waterfall.

Out of the corner of my eyes, I realized there were millions around me. It woke me from my sleep, and I jumped out of bed so quickly, I landed on the floor. Terrified, I ran over to the Bible on the nightstand and tried to read Psalm 91for my protection (yeah, right!). As I read, my eyes seemed like sand in an hourglass as they melted like water in my head and splashed like water on the Bible, which I quickly dropped. Since this time, I have been able to see in the Spirit in a way that goes beyond description. Praise God almighty for His generosity.

But at the time, I was beside myself with fear and ran over to a spot on the floor. I tried to get down on my knees to pray, but was caught up in a whirlwind lifted me off the floor. It seemed I would be caught up to Heaven again, but resisted (and to this day, I regret that). The Holy Spirit whispered inside me, "Go out, go out."

I went to the lobby, and it was the middle of the night. I wanted some tea and found a bellhop in the hallway, who got me a pot of tea for my room. When he returned, I told him I was a Christian who was there for a conference. He readily said He was also a Christian, but backslidden. I looked at him and could see in the Spirit that he was doing drugs. I told him as much, and he replied, "How do you know that?" I replied that the Holy Spirit was showing me, and he said, "My wife is prophetic, too."

Well, well...I wondered if this was what walking with God's was going be like. I was getting excited now. In the morning, my travel companions asked if I would like to visit a pastor they knew in Columbus, Ohio. I wasn't working at the time, so I went with them, not knowing God wasn't finished with me yet!

As we drove to Columbus, I went into an open vision. I saw Jesus in a white robe, wearing a golden crown on his head. I was on my knees in the vision with a white robe, and I also was wearing a golden crown. I was bowing before him, and he turned his head to look at me, seeing me in the natural world while I watched him in this vision. I was seeing both realms at the same time, which, over the years, has constantly happened.

He declared, "I know who you are!" Instantly, the condemnation of the Devil stopped against me as the Lord revealed His Truth. No more could the Devil convince me that God would reject me in the end. Praise Jesus, who is my righteousness. As John 8:36 puts it, "Therefore if the Son makes you free, you shall be free indeed."

We continued to Columbus, and after several hours, the van started making a noise as it went downhill. The sister who was driving pushed on her accelerator, but her van acted as though a giant hand was pushing it back. The van reeled back and forth as it tried to labor down the hill, and everyone immediately started praying out loud. I then saw another vision where thousands of shadow beings shaped like men were running ahead, almost like preparing for an attack. I saw the digital clock on the dashboard read 11:68. I said out loud what I just saw, and Elizabeth said that eight people left Noah's Ark, so the number eight represented new beginnings. She also said that 60 minutes past 11 is 12:00, and so a new day. She then told me perhaps God would do something new? I took her word on that.

We drove for another hour, and the van's tire blew out and went flat. I got out and tried to find the spare in the back; I couldn't find it. I asked the sister driving, and she thought it should be there, but she didn't know anything about vehicles. I looked under the van and saw nothing. Elizabeth told me to try to flag a vehicle to get help.

I went onto the highway with a little reading light, as it was pitch-black dark outside. Even with the moonlight, I realized I couldn't see my hand in front of me. I realized I wouldn't see an animal if it crept up to me, and I felt fear grip my heart.

An 18-wheeler truck started coming down the highway, and he was hauling it. The truck zoomed by, going about 70 miles per hour. I started waving with the light but to no avail. I was out there for about a half-hour when a second truck approached as fast as the first one. I frantically waved my light, and he blew right by me. I turned to see he was several hundred feet past me and was speeding down the highway. I turned and started waving the light, and soon, I heard the truck sounding an alarm as it backed up towards me.

I thought to myself, *But that's impossible because he was racing down the highway* I saw it was a huge, old white truck. I went to the passenger side and climbed onto his steps, telling him our situation. He offered to take me to the next town. So, I went to tell Elizabeth, who told me to get help.

I got in this man's truck, and it slowly moaned as it labored forward. I smelled burning sulfur. "This truck is pretty old," I remarked.

The driver, who had identified himself as James, looked at me and said, "This truck has been in the company a long time!"

As soon as he said the word "company," something resonated in my Spirit, and I couldn't shake it (I was thinking, a company of Angels?).

James soon got up to full speed, and I noticed he was going 60 miles per hour. I checked the time to get an idea of how far was the next town.

James was talking, and I told him I was a Christian. He then started to share that since he drove all over North America, he didn't have time to go to church. He asked if I thought it was okay that he read his Bible in the back cab and prayed there.

I have never wanted to discourage people from seeking God, so I told him, "It's better to seek God than to not."

He seemed very pleased with my answer.

Now, James had long dark hair and a beard. Within a few moments, I noticed something on the shoulder of the road. It appeared to be a man who was a Spirit—I could see through him—and He ran so fast that he ran around to the front of the truck directly in the headlights. He was about six feet tall and looked like a muscular man, and he was somehow staying ahead of us for a few seconds. He then took off in a blink of an eye, and was gone.

I stared for a second, and the thought occurred to me that if I had seen it, surely James had seen it, too. I turned to look at him, and James was staring at me with this huge grin on his face.

Now, this was creepy; for a split second, he looked like Charles Mason. Not saying a word, I turned back to look forward. I spoke silently in my heart, "Heavenly Father, surely he saw it, too? Was it an Angel on the Highway?"

Who was with me in the truck—an angel or the Devil? I couldn't tell, and we spent the next ten minutes or so in an awkward silence.

I saw a Shell gas station coming up, and James told me I could call for help from there. I thanked him and climbed down out of the truck. I walked towards the gas station and could see the truck in the reflection of the huge panes of glass out front. I took only a few steps, and looked up again to see the truck's reflection—but it was gone!

I spun around, looking down the street at a long winding curve that I could see at least several hundred feet away. But the truck had completely vanished.

In complete shock, I made my way inside the gas station. I used the phone to contact state troopers and waited for about forty-five minutes. A state trooper pulled in with my friends following behind them.

When I asked Elizabeth how long it took for the troopers to arrive, she answered ten minutes. She said he'd only taken ten minutes to find the spare under the van, but the sheet metal covering was muddy; when

I had searched for the spare, I couldn't tell it was the bottom. She went on to say that the officer had changed the tire in another ten minutes. So, that had been thirty minutes! James and I had driven for 35 minutes; impossible that they had made the trip with only five minutes to spare.

When the Kingdom of God enters the realm of Earth, the Lord alters time and changes physical laws. Time, gravity, and physics are all but nothing before the Lord (this is the Kingdom of God, as Jesus spoke about to the disciples). Remember that time does not affect God because He lives in eternity and made time for man to mark His days.

As my friends and I drove on, I shared what had happened with James, and everyone was screaming, praising God. Elizabeth then told me that as James and I had pulled away in the truck, she'd looked at the clock, which read 12:08. What? Praise God Almighty.

We arrived late at the pastor's house in Columbus. He and his family were friendly, but somehow, I knew the pastor's life was out of order. They gave me a room to sleep in, but the presence of evil was everywhere in this house. It wasn't his wife or children, but something in the pastor's life had allowed the enemy into the home.

I started praying because seeing demons was different for this new believer. I was asking the Lord to send the chariots of Israel and the horseman thereof. Recently, in the Bible showed me the chariots carried Elijah away. I went to sleep, and in the middle of the night, a dream woke me. In the dream, the Chariots of Fire came down in a whirlwind, spiraling like a tornado; white horses were pulling the chariots made of gold with a fire burning around them. My Spirit man floated upwards out of my body and was hovering vertically above me. The glory around me was brighter than the noonday sun illuminating the area, and I could not see; but somehow, I knew that someone was walking towards me with such Authority.

He said to me, "Peace be still, do not be afraid" as an invisible hand touched my forehead. My Spirit floated back down into my body, and I had the best sleep of my life. It seemed I slept three nights' worth of sleep at once.

Now, I know how Elijah had gone forty days without food after an Angel fed him. God's Kingdom has an abundance to it, where everything is multiplied, sustaining better than any earthly thing. Thank you, Jesus.

I shared my dream with Elizabeth, and she suggested we all pray for protection. As I went to pray, I saw a vision of thousands of these Chariots lined up on both sides of the highway, from Columbus to the Canadian border. I started wondering what God was calling me to do.

When we arrived in Toronto, I remembered something I heard the Holy Spirit whispering to me as we'd driven to Baltimore. "YOU SHALL NEVER BE THE SAME."

So, it begins.

# EVANGELISM

I wanted to separate this section from the normal workings of church life to illustrate what happens when the believer practices what he preaches to the world.

We had a visitor at the church to speak. Our senior pastor was named Julie, who heard God very clearly. The guest speaking was a preacher from an area in Toronto known for having a large black population.

I gave this man of God a drive home after service. As we drove for some time, we saw a basketball court full of black men playing. There was also a court full of Filipino men. I commented that I should go over there to tell them about Jesus.

The preacher said, "Boy, they ain't going to let some white boy go there to talk to them."

His words surprised me because we're all brothers and sisters regardless of where our family originated.

Something rose in my spirit, and I said to him, "If God wants me to go there, I could go with Him."

I dropped off the man of God (he was worthy of respect). As I returned the same way, I drove by the court. I said within my heart, *I should go there sometime.* The Holy Spirit spoke clearly and loudly to me, "Why don't you go now?" Still, I drove for another twenty minutes debating with God about how I was wearing a white dress shirt and dress pants; however, He just kept convincing my heart and wasn't letting me go. As I approached the corner several blocks from my home, I gave in, saying, "Fine, I'll go!" I shook my head in disbelief, knowing that the Gospel tracks I had with me were about a woman who went to hell and came back. I wasn't sure how relevant or appealing this literature would be to these men.

I arrived at the parking area, quickly saying a prayer. As I saw the court, I could see about twenty men; they had enough players to play with a bench. I approached the first man and asked, "Could I give this track to you and tell you Jesus loves you?" He shook his head no, and so did the second guy as fear gripped my heart. A guy sitting on the bench yelled out, "Who is this cracker?" and let out a loud laugh. The third man was about 6'4" and looked around 240 pounds, wearing a white hat. He seemed to take a step back and nodded yes. He reached for the track!

Instantly, the Heavens opened, and the presence of God came down, filling the courts. All the men started reaching for the track as I approached all of them. I walked across to the other court to approach the other group of men. They also started taking the tracks and saying, "Thank you!"

I drove home, stunned by what had happened. Arriving, I sat on the steps praising God for what He had done in about two hours. Is this what He can do? Well, I was excited about the next adventure.

The Book of Acts probably describes my life well after God touched me with His Holy Spirit. I spent years giving prophetic words and sharing visions with people everywhere. Too many to count, but I will share some more here.

I remember going to sleep one night and having a dream. In the dream, I came to some rocks and laid my head on them like pillows. I saw a ladder that reached Heaven. Jesus walked towards the ladder in Heaven and looked down, saying, "Come up here!"—just like Jacob's ladder. Since that time in those visions, in churches—or anywhere for that matter—I will see stairs reaching to Heaven and hear a voice call unto me, "Come up here," showing it is always higher in God's kingdom. God also showed me visions of things in His Kingdom that reveal everything written in the Bible still exists somewhere in Heaven.

God is continually bringing in the Spirit to see scriptures, and the places still exist today. Do people seriously doubt that His Word is relevant today? No one will be able to change anything He has written. In my visions, I saw a table in Heaven with a Bible on it, and as I walked by, it was glowing with a golden light of God's Shekinah glory, brighter than the noon day's sun. The Lord would then bring scripture into my heart, and He would breath on it to become a living Word, its meaning revealed instantly. To me, there was no mistaking what He said, but I will see Christians arguing about Doctrine and remain quiet as they wrestle with God's truth. It has happened several times over the years.

I also recall one evening at a Wednesday night service at a church I was attending named The Guiding Light. I was a deacon by now, though had been out of work for some time; however, I had keys to this church. The service drew to an end, and a man came in to sit at the back. He was about 6'6". An elder asked if he needed anything, and the man yelled that he didn't. I could tell the families wanted to leave, and as this man seemed very drunk, the elder asked him to leave, which he refused to do.

I told the elder he could go, and I would lock up the church. With some persuading, I convinced the drunk man to leave for a coffee. I told him I would drive, so to the coffee shop we went.

On the way to the coffee shop, the man asked me if I thought Jesus would forgive all our sins. I replied yes, to which he replied, "Even murder?" My friends, you know what I was thinking now—*Lord, do I have an ax murderer in my car?*

We went on to talk about God's forgiveness of anything if you gave Him your heart. We parked by the coffee shop, I wondered what was preventing this giant of a man from giving his heart right then and there to Jesus. We knelt on the road together, and this man invited Jesus into his heart. Praise God! Like so many people I've encountered over the years, I never saw this man again. How is it we believers cross the path of thousands, only never to see them again? God knows the answer.

The church started asking me to preach on Wednesday nights. This was a big step, and I thought God was moving me to my full-time ministry. Instead, after one service, I felt the tangible presence of God come into the room. Over the next week, several people commented to the senior pastor how they felt this same presence as well. I was brought before the pastor, who accused me of thinking I was higher in the church than the role I served. I heard the Lord tell me, "Don't say a word but remain silent."

At that point, I learned what prophetic people would tell me: that you come to a place where the church rejects you. The Lord was preparing me for the most challenging twenty-five years of my life.

One night, just weeks before I accused in the church I was attending, I had a dream, and behold, there was a stairway that went from earth to Heaven. It had white steps and golden hand rails. I approached to go up the stairs, but an Angel about twenty feet tall stood before me. The Angel was clothed in a white robe. He pointed to his right and I heard him say, "That's not the way, but this is the way." I turned to look, and beheld a giant wilderness in the dark night, full of forests that could be seen in the moonlit sky. The next words I heard come out of my mouth were "That's huge."

Instantly, I knew that the wilderness was trials, troubles, and tests that were coming my way. God wasn't going to let me just go up the stairs to Heaven, but had another way in mind. Places God would say, "Not many people would go through all of this." Where men dare not tread.

# The Wilderness

For the next twenty years, I was married and raised children. I worked 3.5 years in Toronto as a steamfitter. My wife and I saw the Toronto Vineyard Revival start, which we attended several times. I also went to Deeper Life Church, which was Pat Francis's ministry. We went to Edmonton and ended up working to provide for my family. It seemed like we were always on the outside, looking in at every church we went to attend. Furthermore, it always seemed like the pastor chose favorites to attend their church, never asking the Lord whom He chose.

So, I started doing more outside the churches everywhere I went, including job sites and donut shops. I approached people from every walk of life, talking to them about Jesus. I probably prayed for at least 10,000 people, and at this time, my wife decided she wanted a divorce. All the time I'd spent working away from home had taken its toll on her.

But what about God's destiny for me? I want to share a testimony of God's goodness. We attended an African church for about two years. There were First Nations people who came in together. One brother introduced himself as Al from Hobbema, a reserve south of Edmonton. He was asking church leaders to go to the reserve and pray with the people there. He became discouraged and asked me if I would like to come. Well, the Lord had told me months earlier that he would send me to the First Nations people. So I readily agreed to visit, and Al and I made plans.

I only had every other weekend off. So, two weeks later, I left early on a Thursday because it had started snowing. I had bald tires on the car and was about to travel on a highway with only two lanes going to Edmonton, which was five hours away. As I was going home, my car went out of control, skidding onto the oncoming lane. Snow sprayed across my windshield, and I was completely blind. I looked in my rearview mirror to see a car approximately 100 feet behind my vehicle. I screamed out, "Jesus!", and my automobile turned, heading back across the other side.

As I was crossing my lane, I could not help but notice the vehicle behind me was still only 100 feet away. My car slid towards the shoulder and went off the road. Immediately, I saw the road was roughly twenty-five feet above a field, and was sloped at a 45-degree angle. As my vehicle went over the edge, I grabbed the steering wheel and said, "Brace for impact." I turned to stare out my passenger side window, and then I turned to look back at the windshield. My car was driving at a 45-degree angle parallel to the road. I looked at the speedometer, and it was going eighty kilometers per hour.

The car and I went from going downward with gravity to being transported elsewhere in the blink of an eye. I never saw the vehicle skid or turn ninety degrees. My head was still facing downward on the slope as God moved the car and me in the other direction. I clung to the steering wheel with two tightly gripped hands. The car filled entirely with God's voice, and He said, " Turn towards the road!" I slowly edged the steering wheel toward the road so the vehicle made slight movements back onto the highway. I drove onto the road about 400 feet south, and then I saw the other car about 200 feet back.

I was in utter astonishment and shock. I could not believe what had just happened. My car couldn't hold onto the road, but God had made it drive on a 45-degree angle in snow for about 400 feet, all while the car had bald tires? Praise God, who is not limited by physical laws, time, space, or anything that constrains mankind.

As I drove for the next five minutes, I looked in the rearview to see the car trailing me about two miles behind. I don't think He wanted to go anywhere near me, given how impossibly I had returned to the road. Praise God. This incident shows me beyond anything else that God is Almighty, transporting the car and me back onto the road.

I arrived home and could not wait to see what God would do for the First Nations people. God did not disappoint. I arrived on Saturday to meet with Al in Hobbema. He told me to leave my car at a Tim Horton's, and Al would drive me to the reserve. As we drove past the sign entering the reserve, I heard myself declare as the words almost forced themselves out of my mouth, "I have come to do your will, oh Lord, out of the volume of your book it is written of me."

The power of God hit me, and Al turned to look at me and asked, "Why did you say that?"

I replied that I didn't know. Only God knows the answer to that still.

We went to Al's home, and he asked me to pray with several family members. As soon as I started praying, the entire ceiling lit on fire, which I didn't see in the Spirit; instead, I felt the flames physically burning against my flesh. It was as though I was standing next to a campfire, the heat blazing against my face.

When Al and I finished at his home, I didn't want our prayers to end because I was going through a tough time. We went to meet his friends at a woman's house. As I started praying, the fire returned, blazing once more. Prophetic words began pouring out of my mouth, and several First Nations people went to ask Al why he'd told me personal details about them. I heard him reply that I had not told him anything. One woman exclaimed, "Why does he know all these things about us?"

"I don't know," Al told them. Well, praise God for the prophetic.

Unfortunately, Al started working as a teacher again, and the door closed. So sad, as I'd thought God would set these people free.

Another of God's visits happened when I first came to a church in Stony Plain, Alberta. The Lighthouse Church had a group from Bethel Church called the Fire Starters, who teach everyday believers to operate in the gifts.

I sat down amongst about 300 people attending. As soon as I sat, God spoke clearly to me, "Watch this!" I looked around, wondering what He meant by that statement. The leader of this group was preaching, so he asked if there was any sick among us. He instructed everyone who was sick to stand up, telling everyone here that they are the body and should pray for each other.

I had back issues from working in construction. So I stood, and a man came to pray for my back. I saw a vision of two angels on either side of my feet. Flames shot out under me, and two small Angels were fanning the fire on my feet. I told the man praying what I saw, and he said, "You have an anointing for praying for peoples' feet." I knew feet represented evangelism, but did not want to argue with him. The church was asking for testimonies, and this gentleman proclaimed, "This man has an anointing for foot problems." The Fire Starter leader then yelled out, "This man has an anointing to pray for foot problems."

I don't know how I'd gotten myself into this, but people started lining up beside me, and I started to pray for them. After about ten minutes, I looked up to see about 100 people standing to receive prayers from me. I saw the senior pastor tell the ushers to catch people if they collapsed under the power. As it was my first visit to this church, I can't tell you how this experience came about except God telling me "Watch this." He has quite a sense of humor.

I still don't know if my healing touched people or not because during the wilderness years, I didn't get to find out. I had thousands of visions for believers and unbelievers alike; words of knowledge, discernment, and prophecy. People would give some feedback, but probably 80 percent wouldn't tell me the results of my prophecies. The Lord kept what happened to everyone from me, too; I guess because it would humble me. After twenty-five years in the wilderness, I know without a doubt that only God can do miracles, and I will not touch His Glory.

I will share one more testimony here. God had shown me miracles, signs, and wonders during these twenty-five wilderness years. I still, to this day, cannot understand how I did not find my destiny.

I was friends with an apostle named Alex from Bill Hamon's network of apostles and prophets. We would have coffee, and he would try to encourage me in the ways of God. The church he and his wife ran was called Joseph's Storehouse in Edmonton. They invited a speaker from Christian International, who was internationally known. Alex told me that when this minister would go to countries, palace guards and secret service men from governments asked this man to stand before dignitaries, as his words from the Lord always came to pass.

In time, this minister came to preach to us. I already was going through many trials over ten years, and not eager to endure more. The man started praying for me, and he didn't get anything. I saw Alex nodding his head, indicating he believed the prophet would say something. I moved forward when this man turned and grabbed my shoulder, saying, "God, I see an apostolic release coming on this man later in life."

I did not expect the next fifteen years to worsen, being tested in more trials, but they did. As prophetic people point out, sometimes things get worse after the vision is revealed, bringing attack. Currently, I do not know how I made it except the grace of God. The fifteen years leading up to this time were beyond what I could have imagined.

I know people say that God will not tempt you beyond what you are able to bear without making a way to escape. But I can tell you that if there is a way to escape, the Lord does not have to bring you out until you have finished what he started. As Luke 12:48 states, "For everyone to whom much is given, from him much will be required, and to whom much has been committed of him they will ask the more."

I will share one more story. My daughter Naomi was attending Bible camp. I went to the Holy Spirit night on Wednesday night at our church. Everything was going well that week, and on Friday, I had to pick up Naomi. Sometimes you feel so full of the Spirit that you minister from the overflow, and such was this day.

On my way to the camp, I drove down the highway and saw a man hitchhiking. Rain had started to fall, so I felt for him and stopped to ask where he was going. He said he was going to Busby, Alberta. As it turned out, I had to pass Busby to get my daughter. I offered him a ride, and immediately noticed he was drunk. He told me he was Rowdy Roddy Piper, though I knew that was the name of a wrestler from years back. He then said his name was Roddy.

I always made it a habit that if a hitchhiker got in my car, I would tell them about Jesus. I started sharing, and all of a sudden, he asked me if Jesus could forgive us our sins. I told him that's what we believe, and as I was speaking, the Holy Spirit spoke clearly to me, telling me that this man had a problem with his knee. I asked Roddy if he had a knee problem. He said he did, with both knees, so I asked him, "Roddy, how it is a perfect stranger could tell you about an injury without knowing him?"

"I don't know," he replied, and leaned in the passenger seat towards me, almost enough to put his head on my shoulder. "Who told you?"

I started to say to him the Lord was showing me, and his eyes went bug-eyed. He leaned away from me towards the passenger side window, and I wondered if he was going to open the door and roll out of the car. But Roddy then proceeded to pour out his heart, that he was backslidden and had left the church in Toronto. He said it had been a Salvation Army church, and his brother, a captain, was in charge of the congregation.

He admitted he was drinking and had ended up on the street.

We traveled to Busby, talking the whole way. When we arrived, I pulled over and asked him if I could pray for him. I prayed over his knees and put my right hand on his shoulder. Suddenly, I saw Jesus step out of me in a vision from the top of my head to the bottom of my feet. It was as if I was his body, and he stepped out of me to minister to this man.

Col 1:27: "To whom God would make known what is the riches of the Glory of this mystery among the Gentiles; which is Christ in you, the hope of Glory."

The Lord moved towards the center of the seats, and I watched him wrap His arms around this man's neck. Roddy started weeping like an infant, lifting his head to heaven and crying out, "Lord, forgive me for what I have done."

He got out and retrieved his bag from the backseat. He had the back door open with tears running down his cheeks and kept saying, "Thank you, thank you." I screamed, "Praise to the Lord that gives men the chance to see His Glory!" I thanked Him over and over as I drove to get my daughter.

I'm on a roll now, so I'd better share one more. A friend named Bob would go places with me, and we would see what God wanted to show to us. We must have prayed for about 100 sick people that year. I had Stephen, my son, in the car with me. We went by a grocery store, and I noticed a man coming out with a walker. I felt the Holy Spirit pull on my heart as He likes to do when you see someone in need.

So, we approached what appeared to be a First Nations man with a walker that had an oxygen bottle. He sat down to rest in front of the store. I told him my name was Shawn and introduced Stephen to him. He told us his name was Norman. I said I was a Christian and wanted to know if I could pray for him. He said he was residing in an outpatient hospital named Good Samaritan. I laid my hand on his chest and started to pray for his lungs to be healed. Immediately, his throat appeared to me in the Spirit, and I placed my hand on his throat to pray for it. Then, the Holy Spirit showed me his liver, and I prayed for it, putting my hand on the left side of his stomach. The Lord then told me he was troubled in his mind, and I placed my hand on his forehead.

As I stood up straight, Norman began to shake his head, saying, "You're pretty in touch with your Spirit; I didn't tell you anything. You prayed for my throat, and they give me medication for it because oxygen dries it out. You prayed for my liver, and I have hepatitis C, affecting my liver."

I asked him if his mind was troubled. He replied, "No, my mind is not troubled."

The Holy Spirit then spoke again so clearly, it was almost audible: "He is lonely." I loudly declared, "He says you're lonely."

Norman said that was right, and started laughing. I put my hand on top of his head and saw a vision of an old lady coming into the room. I prophesied that God would send an old Christian woman as a nurse to be a friend to him.

Norman starts laughing, saying, "It was nice meeting you! God is so good, and I thank him."

# The Place of Angels

It is one thing to wonder if the truck that picked me up in Columbus involved an angel. I shared how I saw two angels fanning flames on my feet. I shared how a twenty-foot angel spoke to me in my dream that I was going into the wilderness. God uses angels to do many things to protect us, watch over us, and deliver messages to us.

Aramaic Bible in English Psalm 104:4: "He makes his angels the wind and his ministers burning fire."

I have heard ministers tell me this verse means that God sets his ministers (people) on fire. I can only talk about what God shows me in visions and visitations; I won't listen to the doctrine of men. I have believers tell me about scriptures and what they mean, and yet, I have God show me the same verses in Heaven with revelations. No wonder there is so much division in the church. These ministering angels look like the shapes of men at different heights, their features are sometimes totally engulfed in flames, and you cannot see where their eyes, nose, or mouth are supposed to be. They are a complete pillar of fire, and you can see facial features, but just in outline. They appear in meetings or wherever believers are to assist their heirs of salvation. I have a perfect example from when I was working on the shutdown of a plant.

We went for lunch, and I sat by an apprentice who I knew was a Baptist. I know sometimes people have problems with the supernatural, yet I was pumped up in the joy of the Lord. I started telling him about "Christ in you, the hope of Glory." I went into 2 Cor 4:7: "But we have this treasure in earthen vessels, that the excellence of the power may be of God and not us."

I was literally on a roll as scripture started pouring from my lips, and all of a sudden, a pillar of fire appeared beside us; yet, this time I didn't see it as a vision but felt its physical presence beside my left leg. It was like being beside a roaring campfire, to the point that my leg was burning from the nearness.

I spoke for several more seconds, but my brain was rapidly firing at what was taking place. We turned towards the table as I said, "By the way, there is an angel in a pillar of fire standing right there" as I pointed to the location. "You probably think I'm crazy!" I said.

"No," he replied," I felt it, too, Shawn, and it's standing right there!" as he looked at the exact location.

What? Now people are feeling the manifestations, too. Praise God, this is getting exciting. The look of astonishment on his face at that moment was priceless!

Another time, I was visiting to see Sharon Stone (a minister, not the actress). Everyone was worshipping and having a great time. Instantly, two angels appeared at my feet, one on either side. They were spinning like cyclones. The angels are like tornados, and the ministers of flame are like pillars of fire. I see them more and more, especially during these times. As a man sows, so shall he reap.

Galatians 6:8: "But he that sows to the Spirit shall reap everlasting life."

Another scripture is relevant to what I want to share with other believers—Matthew 13:12: "For whoever has, to him more will be given, and he will have abundance; but whoever does not have, even what he has shall be taken away from him."

If we believers do not use what God has given us, we lose it. Now, I know the gifts and calling of God are given without repentance, but most believers sit in pews because they fear man more than God. He who faithfully uses the talents God gave him will find the Lord adding to them, and there is no limit to His kingdom; He will give more to him who has. So, brother and sisters, start stepping out in faith, believing that He that began a good work in you will finish it until the day of Christ Jesus.

Now is the right moment to hear about the school of the supernatural visiting a church in Cochrane, Alberta. The Lord told me to start small and join a small group; He told me not to despise small beginnings, which as He told me, would spring me into the supernatural at a greater level.

For almost thirty years, I have always prayed every day for at least 1.5 hours, knowing I can do nothing without the Lord. As I prayed for the Lord to be with the team that day, I saw a vision of a white pick-up truck stop on Highway 2 going to Cochrane. Three men got out of the vehicle, and I recognized them as angels. They walked to the back and, on the tailgate, they lay wood logs approximately six feet long inside the box of the truck. They were in a pyramid formation, with around six on the bottom until there was only one at the top.

Flames engulfed the logs, with fire shooting up into the air at least twenty feet high. The fire also touched the truck, and I heard the Lord say that I would receive that day.

When we arrived at the church, we formed a circle and started praying when I saw the back door slam open as a wind blew into the church. I remember thinking during this vision, *Okay, something is going down this weekend.*

We ministered for Saturday and Sunday as usual, then headed home in the afternoon. My friend asked the pastor's wife to prophesy on him when everyone was done. We were already ministering for about an hour and a half when she flowed prophetically for thirty minutes. Everyone had left except only a few people. I looked around, waiting because I was my friend's ride. "Where is what you told me would happen, Lord?" I asked to myself.

Suddenly, I saw a man I knew was an Angel across the room. In a vision, he walked towards me. I could see in the Spirit and the natural world simultaneously as he came right beside me. He turned around and started walking beside me in lockstep. He mimicked everything I did, and he was staring directly at me.

He walked with me like soldiers who march together, moving their arms together in the same motion.

Then, I heard the Lord clearly say to me, "From this time forward, he shall remain with you!"

Since then, I have listened to him tell me an angel the size of an apartment building spinning like a tornado will go with me across the continent. I also saw an Angel who looked like lightning strike the ground from a white cloud about eight feet off the floor in our home. The Lord told me this new angel was going with me in ministry (this one moves in the miraculous). *Okay, Lord, I'm willing for you to send as many Angels as you can. Let's see what you want to do, Father.*

We were praying for a sick friend when I saw the lightning-like angel appear behind her with his striking features (no pun intended). I heard the Lord say that he moves in the miraculous. I told my friend that I saw this angel, and what the Lord declared. As soon as I started praying, her entire body become outlined with what appeared to be a ½-inch line of light. The presence of power began to reverberate around both of us, and it pulsated through us, praying for healing. She received some healing that day.

I have noticed that whenever I shared God's Glory with someone, His presence comes into the room. When I shared testimonies with one friend for about two hours, angels started coming in through the door one after another; they lined up wearing white robes and carrying silver swords. There was a golden hue shining with the shekinah glory of God throughout the room.

As we share testimonies, the same presence of Glory comes as it does when He reveals himself. Suppose we speak of a healing testimony or God's intervention in our lives; the same angels and His heavenly host return who were there during the visitation.

The same anointing comes with testimony that gives God glory. That is why it is very important to share what God has done. Amen!

# Visions of the Lord

Since I received Him, God has done many things while I have worked as a tradesman for thirty-four years. When I was twenty-five years old, I thought I would be in full-time ministry, but watched what goes on in churches in anguish, not seeing any power, and wondering where is the God of Elijah.

I will share some visions of the Lord to encourage others to contend for the things of God.

One Sunday service, we were worshipping God and enjoying the music. All of a sudden, I saw Angels in white robes carrying golden swords. Immediately, Jesus came walking into the altar area through a door that appeared out of nowhere. He walked across the pulpit area, and the Angels rushed into formation—three on one side and three on the other. They held their swords up as soldiers do to honor a king as he walks by them.

Instantly, when I behold him, my Spirit understood majesty; you know who he is when you look at him. No wonder the elders in John's vision threw their crowns at the Lord's feet! People try to understand how Angels worship him day and night, but prophetic believers understand that God has different revelations of His glory. We are constantly learning who the Father is.

Speaking of the Lord revealing Himself, I was worshipping at the little storefront church from years before in Toronto. Suddenly, I saw the Lord standing by the wall in a vision. He had long dark hair and a beard, and was wearing a white robe. Instantly, I was in Heaven and could see the river of life rushing by me on the right side as I looked towards the Lord standing in the same place. I could see His eyes, and out of them came a wave in the Spirit towards me. His Love surrounded me, and I could feel the physical manifestation of His presence. The peace that surpasses understanding filled my being, gratifying every need in my life.

I saw His hand stretch twenty feet through the air towards me and go through my chest. He clasped his hand around my heart and gently tugged on it. I physically felt my heart moving in my chest, and I heard him say, "Come to me." In this vision, I exploded into praise, overwhelmed by what was happening.

I will never forget this vision as long as I live. Praise Jesus now and forever. God wants you to seek Him, my friends. The Father's heart longs to spend time with you as He asks you to come to him!

We visited a church with the school of the supernatural in Fort Saskatchewan, Alberta. During worship, the Lord of Glory Jesus Christ appeared in front of the singers. In this vision, he wore a white robe with a golden crown on his head, watching everyone worship him. He looked around the room, as if looking into the worshippers' hearts.

When parents see something they like from their children, they take a picture with their camera. The Lord sees someone worshipping him, and removes his crown from his head. He captures the moment forever by snapping it into his crown like an ornament. Jesus, the Spirit of God, thus revealed to me he can remember that exact time you touched his heart with your worship.

It is written that God dwells in the praises of His people. In this meaning, we should take worship so much more seriously.

"You shall be a crown of glory in the hand of the Lord." - Isaiah 62:3

God will remember your praises.

# Visions of God's Promises

I will share some dreams and visions to illustrate how God kept me going for thirty years of not seeing His promises.

When I was about seven years old, my mother and I were walking past a nursing home. She told me that her grandmother was a Mi'kmaq

First Nations person—people in eastern Canada call them Mic Mac Indians. She shared how her grandfather was of French descent, and his wife became pregnant. There were complications, and while they tried to deliver the child with forceps, they tore the baby to pieces. Her grandmother could not take the grief and hung herself.

My mom didn't remember saying this years later, but her story sticks with me to this day. I asked her why this happened, and she replied, "Because of the hatred of people towards the First Nations people."

All of a sudden, a vision came to me of a dove flying out of heaven made of golden light. The dove flew into my chest, just like the Holy Spirit when Jesus was baptized. When it flew into me, I was instantly knit with all First Nations people, finding a love for them everywhere I meet them. Whenever I see them, I also see a shift in the Spirit and go from operating in the prophetic realm to the apostolic one, not only seeing prophecies come to pass but the working of miracles still waiting for the fulfillment of God's promises of destiny.

I also have a cautionary tale of how some Christians can try to label you. I dreamt one night that I was in a subway station where there used to be dozens of phones lined up for people to make calls (obviously from the '90s). I was frantically putting change into the phones and getting a busy signal. I went from one phone to another, trying but nothing, knowing how phone calls represent prayers to heaven in dreams.

I made quite a few calls, and somehow helped someone who wanted to commit suicide along the way. I ran out of change because this was not a short dream; rather, it was so clear, it had vibrant colors and remarkable details. I went into the store and asked for change, giving the man at the counter a bill. When I looked down for coins, I found nothing but lint from a pocket with old buttons. Immediately, I knew the storeowner was Satan, and he was trying to deceive me from what I wanted to accomplish. I became bold and commanded him, "Give me what is mine!" As I went back to the phones, I turned the corner and saw one single phone booth.

I put my last coin into the slot and tried to call. Instantly, coins, silver, and gold came rushing into a bin under the phone, filling it to overflowing. A young man and woman tried to muscle me away from this answer from heaven, but I resisted them. Then, I said to them, "It's mine, and I'm giving it back to who it belongs."

I believe after thirty years of waiting, I will see the fulfillment of this dream. The many calls represent how many trials I have been through the years, while the changing of the money is the enemy trying to keep me from our inheritance. The young people were Satan's demons trying to stop me. The silver and gold was God's answer to destiny—giving him Glory when I give it back to him. God is not finished with you yet, my friends.

In the early '90s, I dreamt that Benny Hinn came into our meeting at the church. He called me up to lay his hands on me, and sent me sprawling to the floor as power overcame my body. At the time, I wondered why I dreamt this, but years later, I dreamt that I saw Benny again in his ministry headquarters. I approached him and immediately put out my right arm with my palm upward. He greeted me and kept talking as he came over to me. Taking a silver knife-type instrument, he scraped my right arm. He returned to his chair and put the sample on what looked like a black stone thing. He added chemicals to the scrapings, the way they do to test gold for karats.

He was making conversation when he suddenly exclaimed, "You're gold—pure gold!" I looked over to see gold spread across the stone. He stood again, coming over to me, and lay his hand on my stomach (where the Spirit is located). He started praying for me, and I turned my head to see thousands waiting to be next. *Why is he taking so long with me?* I wondered in the dream. Again, God's plan showing itself can take years of hardship and pain beyond belief before you see its completion. Stay faithful!

A week later, I dreamt I saw Benny for the third time. We were in his house, and he was talking about the countries he has visited. I had also visited those places in my dream (though this still has not come to pass). He also commented on names of ministers he knew, and in the dream, I knew them, too. Again, in the natural world, I have not met these ministers yet, but God is faithful until the end.

Amen! God will speak and confirm His plans and purposes to you, my brothers and sisters.

# 2021

After thirty years of waiting for God's promises, I was walking through a shop at work. It was light from Heaven shining down around my body. I heard the Lord declare, "I'm going to promote you!" He also told me that one day, "You are going to change careers."

Fear gripped my heart, thinking I would retire in three years and find His will. How would I pay for my family's needs? But in 2021, everything starts coming together, almost as if accelerating at an incredible pace.

One morning, I was praying to hear him say, "You will be in ministry within six months." On May 13th of 2021, God says as I arise for work, "Write your book!" On May 23rd, he reiterates to me as I wake, "Be obedient."

I started writing and get laid off the next week. I wrote every day, telling the Lord, "I don't have money or anybody to publish this book." I see a vision of Sid Roth, and the Lord says to send the book to him, and he will help you get it printed! The rest is in God's Hands.

# Conclusion 2021

I was in Edmonton talking to a sister about our getting involved in a relationship. The next day, after praying, she said we should just remain friends. Being disappointed, I went into the house. I wanted to pray before going out, and I was very tired after working a lot of shifts for twenty days. My flesh was very tired. I don't like praying when I am this tired, but I would try anyway.

I immediately sensed a presence in the living room where I knew someone was in the house with me—someone who reached the sixteen-foot ceiling. I did not see this messenger of God, as I usually do in a vision, but felt the atmosphere change. I went from being extremely weary to being totally alive in the Spirit of God. I was caught up by a power that moved my prayer, as words seemed to form on my lips. For an hour and a half, the words that came were, "Whether she says yes or no, you must go." I stated this happened five times. What an exhilarating and terrifying thing to happen, as I was being warned of the seriousness of the call of God. Almighty God left me awestruck as I prayed in a completely different realm.

Months after this mighty Angel came to speak to me, I thought about this experience. All of a sudden, I heard the Lord speak these words almost audibly in my spirit, "He is your guardian Angel." I was totally shocked, and all can say is, "Here I am Lord, what do want me to do?"

-Shawn

www.ingramcontent.com/pod-product-compliance
Lightning Source LLC
LaVergne TN
LVHW090125160826
845673LV00015B/1016

* 9 7 8 1 7 3 8 7 0 3 1 0 4 *